AN INTRODUCTION TO

POPULAR CONSCIENCE

HUSSAIN'S REVOLUTION

AYATOLLAH MUHAMMAD MAHDI

CHAMSEDDINE

THE MAINSTAY
FOUNDATION

Author: Ayatollah Muhammad Mahdi Chamseddine

Translated and Edited by: The Mainstay Foundation

© 2018 The Mainstay Foundation

Printed in the United States.

ISBN: 978-1943393503

CONTENTS

ABOUT THE AUTHOR

Ayatollah Sheikh Muhammad Mahdi Chamseddine was a prominent Shia-Lebanese religious scholar, intellectual, and public figure. He was one of the founders of the Supreme Shia Islamic Council in Lebanon, along with Sayyid Musa Al-Sadr and others. Chamseddine and Sadr were heavily involved in preaching a moderate understanding of Islam that espoused plurality and coexistence at a time when Lebanon was going through an extreme period of violent civil war. After the disappearance of Sadr in 1978, Chamseddine rose to the forefront as his successor.

Chamseddine was not only a religious figure, but a public intellectual and political thinker. He led Lebanon in its national and political introspection, always calling for inter-faith and intra-faith dialogue. He made the unity and advancement of Lebanon his priority through his calls for civic engagement, national sovereignty, and resistance to occupation. At the same time, his theory of political legitimacy was based on notions of social contract and popular sovereignty, as opposed to other prevalent Islamist ideologies at the time. I one of his most influential books *Nidham Al-Hukm Wa Al-Idara fi Al-Islam (The System of Government and Public Administration in Islam)*, Chamseddine set out his theory of national sovereignty based on Islamic teachings that gave religious legitimacy to representative government.

Chamseddine also played a central role in the establishment of the Islamic University of Lebanon, which became a leading institution in the country, including in fields such as surveying and biomedical engineering. The University is a member of the International Association of Universities and the Francophone University Association, as well as a number of other regional associations. Chamseddine also established a number of other institutions, including schools, orphanages, and social service organizations.

Chamseddine was born in Najaf, Iraq, in 1936 to a family known for religious and scholarly achievement. His father had migrated to Najaf to pursue his religious studies there. In 1948, while Chamseddine was still 12 years old, his father decided to return to Lebanon. Chamseddine stayed in Najaf to pursue his own religious education. During his stay of over 30 years in Iraq, Chamseddine studied with the most prominent Shia religious scholars, including Grand Ayatollah Muhsen Al-Hakim, Grand Ayatollah Abulqasim Al-Khoei, and Grand Ayatollah Muhammad Al-Rouhani. He rose to prominence in Najaf and became a distinguished member of the seminary. In 1969, Chamseddine returned to Lebanon, where he began his illustrious legacy as a public figure. He survived an assassination attempt in 1990 and passed away due to illness at age 65 in 2001.

TRANSLATOR'S PREFACE

It was a great honor to have the opportunity to translate a book for a learned scholar and Muslim thinker such as Ayatollah Chamseddine. The book provided great insight into the movement of Imam Hussain (a) and its impact in changing history. May his soul rest in peace alongside the heroes who he dedicated his life to learn and write about.

Ayatollah Chamseddine dedicated his life's work to the study of the lives of the Holy Prophet's (s) household – especially Imam Ali (a) and Imam Hussain (a) – and the impact they had on Muslim history. His analysis of these personalities relied on detailed historical accounts and historiographic study. From that lens, he left behind a wealth of knowledge on Muslim history and historical analysis. Three of his works on the revolution of Imam Hussain (a) – *Hussain's Revolu-*

tion, The Victors of Hussain, and *The Tragedy of Karbala in the Popular Conscience* — were especially insightful and impactful. The first two of these books were translated by the Mainstay Foundation and published in 2016. The latter, however, did not lend itself to translation.

Ayatollah Chamseddine's *The Tragedy of Karbala in the Popular Conscience* is a valuable work on how Imam Hussain's (a) stance in Karbala changed Muslim history by seeping deep into the collective and individual Muslim conscience. The work studies the history of commemorating that tragedy — through visitations of the tomb and shrine of Imam Hussain (a), recitation of poetry dedicated to the tragedy, narration of the detailed events of that movement, and persistent weeping in remembrance of that catastrophe.

The book focused on how the tragedy of Karbala had a direct and lasting impact on Muslims of that time and throughout history. The books focus was mostly limited to the study of these phenomena in Arabic culture — perhaps by the author's design or perhaps due to restrictions of language. And since Arabic is a very poetic culture, the book encapsulated endless verse and prose that did not lend themselves to translation. A full translation of the book would only result in a product too mired in the complications of linguistic differences.

Still, Ayatollah Chamseddine was able to capture the essence of the book in an introduction that laid out his arguments and study concisely. The booklet that is now in the reader's hands is a translation of that introduction. We hope that our readers find its contents a valuable addition to the Ayatollah's other translated works.

Before our readers begin on the journey of this book, we hope that they keep a few important points in mind.

Firstly, there are great structural differences between the original Arabic language of the book and the modern English language. Such structural differences make the task of literal translation burdensome and creates a final result that does not accurately capture the spirit and readability of the Arabic text. Because Ayatollah Chamseddine's work could not be encapsulated in a direct or literal translation, our translation method had to be oblique. Adaptations were used freely to capture the meaning of the text without being bogged down in the structural differences of the two languages.

The process of translation always begs us to find precise meanings for the passages that we translate. But when we encounter the majesty of the Holy Quran, we find ourselves incapable of understanding its intricacies, let alone translating its true and deep meanings. We turned to the works of translators who have attempted to do this before. Although no translation can do justice to the Holy Quran, we found that the translation of Ali Quli Qarai to be the most proper in understanding when compared to the interpretation of the text as derived by our grand scholars. As such, we decided to rely on Qarai's translations throughout this book, with minor adaptations that allowed us to weave the verses more properly with the rest of the work.

A second great limitation came with translating the narrations of the Grand Prophet Muhammad (s) and his Holy Household (a). Their words are ever so deep and ever so powerful. We attempted to convey these passages to the reader in a tone that is understandable without deviating from the essence of the words of these immaculate personalities. We pray that we were successful in this endeavor.

Finally, we want to take this opportunity to thank you for your support. As students of Islam and as translators of this text, our greatest purpose is to please God by passing along these teachings to others. By picking up this book, you have lent your crucial support to this endeavor. We hope that you will continue your support throughout the rest of this book, and we ask that you keep us in your prayers whenever you pick it up.

The Editorial and Translation Team,

The Mainstay Foundation

INTRODUCTION

In the Name of God the Beneficent the Merciful

We ask:

What is the meaning in attributing the word "eternal" to an individual, a specific event in history, or an amazing innovation brought forth by the human mind or spirit?

We answer:

To feel the unremitting need for return, we go back to the eternal individual. We listen, we read his history, and reminisce over his legend.

In remembering eternal events of history, we revive them in our hearts and minds. We enrich our lives and our entire existence by its simple memory. Through the event and those who made it we light the path of our journeys.

And we return to the everlasting wonders of humanity to quench the thirst of our yearning hearts with truth and beauty.

We ask:

Why has timelessness been written for some individuals, events, or wonders?

We answer:

These individuals, events, and wonders encompassed the meaning of the world's perpetual reality and truth. Scores of people and events have been tainted with falsehood, evil, and fabrication – all of which do not last in people's lives. Mankind has been quick to identify, address, and reject what is wrong or false; and thus, build a self-correcting system that enfranchises advancement and progress.

Some have embraced a narrow sense of reality, which limits that legacy to the span of that individuals' life.

Others have truly encompassed reality in its everlasting state that bonds with the perpetual heart and mind. This bond is eternal because it never fails in meeting the demands of the heart and mind and the aspirations of the human soul.

This is what is manifested so meticulously in the personality of Imam Hussain and his awe-inspiring movement. Hussain is eternal and his revolution everlasting. Back to him and his revolution we return time and time again.

We contemplate every step that he took throughout his life, pondering on its wisdom. In examining his immaculate journey, we reach its very peak – his revolution. We recollect, we seek to understand, and we live every moment of it from its beginning to its very end. We are moved, motivated and inspired. After discovering the meaning of his revolution, we discovered our own identity within it. In it we unraveled parts of our hearts, our souls, our aspirations, and our humanity. We gave our ears to listen closely, and listen we did. We heard call after call that echoed the nobility of humanity and all its virtues. We heard the call.

The secret of this revolution is that it immaculately resonates in every heart and soul. Human affection and sentiment embraces the renaissance and revolution of Hussain without any kind of hesitation. Muslims and non-Muslims alike are inspired and moved by his revolution. More particularly, Shia Muslims have dedicated almost every aspect of their lives to his honor. The cultural, social, ethical, and political identity of the Shia Muslim is owed to the revolution and sacrifice of Imam Hussain.

When you look back at the history of Islam and all the revolutions that took place, the revolution of Hussain is the only one that lives vibrantly in the hearts and minds of Muslims. It is also the only movement that has found a place in the popular conscience of the people, whereby it enriched them and was enriched by them. It enriched people with its mantras, ideas, ethics, and noble goals. People enriched it with their noble stands in honor of the revolution and their principled outlooks throughout history. His revolution became the "Mother of Revolutions" in the history of Islam.

As I mentioned in my book, *Hussain's Revolution: Its Causes and Implications*, "Imam Hussain's revolution spurred the oncoming revolts. It was the first revolution that riled the masses and pushed them towards this long and bloody struggle. It came at a point when the nation's spirit and ambition had faded away."[1]

The revolution of Imam Hussain is distinguished in being the only movement that began only sixty years after the Prophet's migration and continues to live radiantly to this day. It is unique in producing a culture of intellectualism and poetry in honor of the principles of faith and the values of humanity.

---

[1] Chamseddine, *Hussain's Revolution*, 205.

This book is an attempt at studying the revolution of Imam Hussain as it exists in the conscience of the populace.

This piece comes after writing two works of mine. The first work is *Hussain's Revolution: Its Causes and Implications*. This book's fourth edition was printed in Beirut, Lebanon in 1977.[2]

The second work is *The Victors of Imam Hussain*. The first edition of this book was published by Dar Al-Fikr in Beirut in 1975.[3]

With the grace of God, this book will be followed with a fourth book titled, *The Story of the Revolution*.[4] By that it will complete the study of the revolution of Imam Hussain in all its primary dimensions. After that we will be free, by the will and grace of God, to study the later revolutions that were inspired by the revolution of Imam Hussain. As we said in *Husain's Revolution*, studying the history of Islam by way of examining its revolutions and movements gives a more accurate picture than the traditional method that

---

[2] *Hussain's Revolution: Its Causes and Implications* was translated and published by the Mainstay Foundation in 2016. –Eds.

[3] *The Victors of Imam Hussain* was translated and published by the Mainstay Foundation in 2016. –Eds.

[4] Unfortunately, Ayatollah Chamseddine did not get around to writing and publishing *The Story of the Revolution* before he passed away in 2001. –Eds.

would only look at either the dynasties or the ruling families.

We ask God to accept our humble work and to allow others to benefit from it. All praise be to Him, the Lord of the Worlds.

Mohammad Mahdi Chamseddine

Explaining the Connotation

Revolution is an event in a certain time and place, having political, social, and economic reasons for pushing a group of people to move – with force – against their current establishment. This could be because the establishment represents a deviation from the people's ideals or that it does not meet the aspirations of this group of people that represent the elites of their nation.

The success, or failure, of the revolution will have certain outcomes. If the revolution is successful, then the norms and institutions of society will change. These institutions and norms will change from what they were before revolution to feature the picture drawn by the revolutionaries – now those who govern – and the slogans they took up during the revolution.

In the case of failure, the establishment will tighten its grip and continue to suppress any movement that challenges the regime's dominance. The establishment would also further entrench its own conceptions in society on all levels of social, economic, and political life.

The failure of a revolution could also, in rare circumstances, move an establishment to change its own conceptions or reform some of its institutions to meet the demands of the revolutionaries. This would be if those in power found that making such amendments would serve the growth and dominion of the establishment. It could be a way to silence the popular discontent against the establishment and disarm them from their weapons of propaganda against the state.

The skeleton – if that is the best illustration – for a revolution is its material events that fall in a certain time and place. This is what is what is generally recorded by history.

However, these events alone – independent from their relationship to the general psyche of the nation, the nation's reaction to the events, and their understanding of such events – have no meaning or significance. In this view, such events would be dead with no life or movement; and thus, they bear no more value to an intellectual than an entertaining story.

The flesh, the veins, and the nerves of these events are represented by how the incidents are seen in the psyche of the public. This is in addition to the reactions of the different groups that are affected by the revolution, as well as the actions that transpire after the revolution takes place.

In this regard, the revolution – whether it succeeds or fails – will be effective and influential in contemporary society. It will naturally take its place in the living history of its nation – a history that is affected by it and affects it. It will endure through time, place, and human life. Its effects will not end with the end of its time or the change of its region, nor with the death of its people.

Revolution in this sense is an actor of change in the nation and is changed or affected by it. It is an actor of change by providing the nation, leaders and followers alike, with models upon which the nation can conform its actions and positions in its movement toward the future.

The revolution is affected by the nation in the way the memory of its events changes in the psyche of the public. The nation itself is influenced by its own psychological outlook on the calamities it experiences and the victories that it achieves. It is possible that the nation will distort the narrative of the events or change some of its components to acclimate to the nation's present interests. Or it may keep the narrative of events unchanged but provide different interpretations of those events to better fit its current status quo. In this situation it would be fundamentally undermining the revolution in its essence to fit its projected interests.

Therefore, it is clear from the aforementioned that history is something alive and well in the public conscious rather than simply being an abstract legend or element of heritage. The relationship between a nation and its history is one of continuous giving and taking – they rely on one another and actively influence each other.

History in this regard is a catalyst for the future and a guiding light for the movement of a nation towards its goals and aspirations. History could very well be a mirror for the present psychological state of the nation and an excuse or justification for its reality that is walking shackled in chains.

It is this outlook of historical events that we call "history in the popular conscience," and what we mean in the title, "The Revolution of Hussain in the Popular Conscience." Through this work we wish to explore how the revolution reflected in people's behavior and positions on issues and events. We further wish to examine the different ways people chose to revive the revolution as well as the extent to which they held on to it. In addition, this work will provide insight to how the events themselves were affected by the psyche and positions of the people, whereby different meanings and new interpretations that were not original or authentic to the revolution were attributed to it.

I hope this work provides a trustworthy illustration of the revolution of Imam Hussain in the popular conscience in the general sense, and to Shia Muslims more specifically.

Positions Towards the Revolution

The Muslims realized the possibility of Imam Hussain's revolution when they witnessed his determination for reform as evidenced in three situations. These situations are to be observed with the reactions of the religious and political leaderships that represented the Muslims of the time.

The Eve of Revolution

The First Position

The first position is manifested by the stance of Ahlulbayt that was adopted by other non-Shia Muslims, for either specific tribal reasons or general political motivations. Their position was to invoke revolution, coupled with promises of victory and positive change in the spirit of reform.

We observe this in the events that followed Imam Hussain's refusal to pay homage to Yazid ibn Muawiya and leaving Medina to head toward Mecca. In fact, we find this even before the death of Muawiya with the efforts of the Kufans at enticing Imam Hussain to revolt, so that he would correct what they perceived as Imam Hassan's error in formulating the peace accord with Muawiya.

After the death of Muawiya, his appointment of his son Yazid to the caliphate, and Hussain's departure for Mecca, the Shia chieftains of Kufa sent Imam Hussain scores of letters of support. Non-Shia chieftains also joined in the campaign of letters to Imam Hussain, calling onto him with support and promoting his revolution. They stood in opposition and boycotted the Umayyad governor of Kufa, Al-Nu'man ibn Basheer Al-Ansari. Instead, the Kufans paid homage to the messenger and representative of Imam Hussain – Muslim ibn Aqeel. Eighteen thousand Kufan men swore their allegiance to Muslim ibn Aqeel in preparation for the arrival of Imam Hussain.

Many of the Kufans remained loyal to their promise to Imam Hussain even after the Umayyads restored their reign over Kufa with the arrival of their new governor – Ubaydillah ibn Ziyad. Ubaydillah relieved Al-Nu'man of his duty as governor and swiftly implemented the fiercest policies over the people of Kufa. People were paralyzed with fear. Many were imprisoned after joining the movement of Muslim ibn Aqeel. Kufa was besieged with ibn Ziyad's troops guarding the city walls, prohibiting them from leaving Kufa to join Imam Hussain in his journey. Very few were able to slip through the weak points of ibn Ziyad's ranks and join Imam Hussain in Karbala. Those few came to his support, fought by his side, and fell as martyrs on the sands of Karbala.

THE SECOND POSITION

The second position is manifested by the words of Muhammad ibn Al-Hanafiyya and Abdullah ibn Abbas. Muhammad ibn Al-Hanafiyya advised his brother Imam Hussain on the eve of his departure from Medina,

> *You leave for Mecca. If you can live there in safety, that's something we would all be happy with. But if that is not the case then go to Yemen. Their people are the supporters of your grandfather, your father, and your brother. They are most gentle and compassionate...[1]*

---

[1] Al-Khwarizmi, *Maqtal Al-Hussain*, 1:187-188.

Imam Hussain received similar advice from Abdullah ibn Abbas in Mecca. In a conversation between Abdullah and the Imam, Abdullah said,

> *I was told that you are heading to Iraq. They are treacherous people. They call you to war, so do not hurry. If you are determined to stand against this tyrant [Yazid] and choose not to remain in Mecca, then go to Yemen. Write to the people of Kufa and your supporters in Iraq to oust their [Umayyad] governor. If they don't then you have your place [in Yemen] until God gives you a further decree. Surely, it [Yemen] has many strongholds and fortifications.[2]*

The position of the non-Hashemites is portrayed by the words of Abdullah ibn Mutee' al-Adwi:

> *I remind you, O' son of the Messenger of God, of God and the sanctity of Islam lest it be abused. I ask you by the sanctity of the Messenger of God. I ask you by the sanctity of the Arabs. For by God, if you are to demand what is in the hands of the*

---

[2] Al-Masoudi, *Murooj Al-Thahab*, 3:64. See also: Al-Khwarizmi, *Maqtal Al-Hussain*, 1:216. It seems that the position of ibn Abbas was a response to Yazid's request of him to stop Imam Hussain from pursuing his revolution. Ibn Abbas replied to Yazid in a meek letter that said, "I hope that Hussain's departure to Iraq is not something that you detest. And I will only give him advice that will unite the nation and quell rebellion." Ibn Asakir, *Al-Tareekh*, 4:221. This supports our view that the relationship the Abbasids had with the Alids (the descendants of Ali) was, from the start, superficial and opportunistic.

*Umayyads they will kill you. They will not hesitate
to kill anyone after you. By God! The sanctity of Islam, the nobility of Quraysh, and the honor of the
Arabs will all be defiled. So, do not do it! Do not go
to Kufa and do not confront the Umayyads.[3]*

These people agreed with the sentiment of the revolution in principle; however, they were fearful of its
consequences. Some of them, like Abdullah ibn Mutee', was certain of its failure. He expressed his
thoughts and feelings of dread and horror of what
would follow the failure of the revolution and the au-
dacity of the Umayyads against everything sacred.
Others were skeptical about the results of the revolution and thus advised to seek haven in places and
communities that would yield greater prospects of
success.

THE THIRD POSITION

The actions and words of Abdullah ibn Umar, and
the "wise" of his likes, portray the third position.[4]
These individuals withdrew from the public discourse
since the assassination of Uthman, with the excuse of
wanting to stay away from sedition. Their position
served the political establishment a great deal in be-

---

[3] Al-Tabari, *Tareekh Al-Tabari*, 5:395-396.
[4] Some of these people included: Anas ibn Malik, Zayd ibn Arqam, and
Al-Hassan Al-Basri.

coming a considerable group that impeded the efforts of revolution and reform under the slogan of piety and distance from sedition.

Abdullah ibn Umar said to Imam Hussain:

> O' Aba Abdullah, I know the animosity that this family [the Umayyads] has towards you and the oppression they put you [and your family] through. The people paid allegiance to this man – Yazid ibn Muawiya. And thus, I wouldn't feel safe of the people's treachery when they are so easily bought by gold and silver. They will kill you. Your actions will lead to the death of many. I recommend that you take the same good course that people have taken and be patient as you have been patient before.[5]

Abdullah ibn Umar and those who shared this sentiment were not followers of Ahlulbayt – they were not Shia. Nor were they of the second group that principally believed in the revolution's just cause. Nor were they, at least on the surface, the employees or agents of the regime. This group looked at the revolution a look of spite derived from a fundamental position they held in their public and private lives. They were content with the status quo and wished to maintain it, not because the current condition was just but be-

[5] Al-Khwarizmi, *Maqtal Al-Hussain*, 1:191.

cause it was simply the status quo. Change or reform did not agree with their dispositions, political attitudes and interests.

AFTER IT WAS OVER

The Muslims took three positions after the tragic end of the revolution and all its consequences of beheadings, captivity and oppression.

THE SHIA

The Shia met the tragic end with sorrow, regret and anger. Their sorrow was a result of the atrocities that took place in Karbala. Their feelings of regret stemmed from their realization of falling short in coming to aid and support Imam Hussain. Finally, their anger was directed at the Umayyad regime for their persistence in committing such a heinous crime.

The combination of sorrow and regret fueled even greater anger within the Shia. From that anger a passionate desire to pay penance was born. That penance was expressed through their opposition to the regime by way of public discourse, symbolic defiance, and revolts that lasted decades. The slogan "Retribution for Hussain" became a slogan for all those who revolted against the Umayyads.

THE MUSLIM MASSES

This position is attributable to the public of Muslims who were not necessarily aligned with the political course of the Shia and the Ahlulbayt. This group reacted to the tragedy of Karbala with shock and condemnation. They were terrified by the nature of Umayyad suppression of the revolution and in their treatment of their political adversaries. Umayyad methods did not respect any system of law or ethics, nor did they bare any weight or recognition for the norms or customs of society.

There is no doubt that this discovery pushed many tribal chiefs and community leaders to reexamine their position towards the Umayyads, as was the case for much of the common people. An example of such individuals was Ubaydillah ibn Al-Hurr Al-Ju'fi. He transformed from a loyalist of the regime who did not answer the call of Imam Hussain, to a revolutionary against the regime eulogizing the martyrs of Karbala and publicly declaring his defiance of the Umayyads.[6]

Even the "wise ones" – those who responded to Hussain's intent for reform with utter coldness and advised him to retreat from his persistence – were unable to stand firm to their initial adverse position

---

[6] Al-Tabari, *Tareekh Al-Tabari*, 5:469-470.

and were instead forced to take up the common public reaction of shock and condemnation.

Zayd ibn Arqam was one of the individuals present in the court of Ubaydillah ibn Ziyad in Kufa. He watched as the captive women of Ahlulbayt were dragged into the court of ibn Ziyad as the lifeless heads of Karbala's martyrs hovered over them on spears held by Umayyad soldiers. Ibn Ziyad had the severed head of Imam Hussain placed in front of him and began to strike it spitefully with a stick. Ibn Arqam broke into tears as he saw ibn Ziyad defile the severed head of Imam Hussain. Ibn Ziyad scolded him for crying and threatened him for his sympathy. Ibn Arqam stood and said,

> O' people, you are slaves after today. You killed the son of Fatima and crowned the son of Marjana.[7] By God, they will kill the good amongst you and enslave the evil of you. Away with those who have accepted humiliation and disgrace![8]

When Al-Hassan Al-Basri heard of the martyrdom of Imam Hussain he said, "Disgraced is a nation that killed the grandson of its prophet…"[9]

---

[7] Ibn Marjana or the son of Marjana was a title of Ubaydillah ibn Ziyad.
[8] Al-Tabari, *Tareekh Al-Tabari*, 5:469-470.
[9] Ibid.

The Regime

The regime and its loyalists responded to these positions by eradicating their opposition of reformers and revolutionaries. They did this with joy and delight. The Umayyads portrayed their feelings through their repulsive leisure and excessive exultance. They did not even try to hide it; instead, their spite led them to ensure that people knew how happy they were with the death of Hussain and his companions.

Yazid especially made a show of his delight with the tragedy. The captive women of Karbala were paraded to the Umayyad palace in Damascus, surrounded by music and dancing.[10] It was a celebration, a festival even, for the Umayyads. As the Prophet's granddaughters were dragged in chains across Damascus, and the severed heads of his grandsons were held on spears, the Umayyads laughed, drank and cheered. Yazid did not hide his utter joy when the captives came into his decorated court and the head of Hussain was placed before him.

This was the case with the rest of the regime's men, like Ubaydillah ibn Ziyad, Marwan ibn Al-Hakam, Amr ibn Saeed ibn Al-Aas, and others. Their joy was

---

[10] Al-Sadouq, *Al-Amali*, 100; Al-Khwarizmi, *Maqtal Al-Hussain*, 2:60.

evidenced by several slogans and sayings recorded in narrations and relayed by historians.[11]

Nonetheless, the regime was quick to learn that the matter at hand was not a laughable matter or something they ought to be happy about. Nor was this endeavor as simple as they had imagined. This revolution was not one that could be effortlessly eradicated and done away with. They soon realized that the supposed failure of the revolution in fact brought to life even greater threats that did not exist before. The entire situation had exploded. The failure of the revolution led the Shia to adopt a more rigid stance as opposed to their more flexible and reconciliatory position previously taken during Imam Hassan's accord with Muawiya. Likewise, the suppression of the revolution changed many Muslims' perspective of the Umayyads. This change in attitude allowed these

---

[11] Amongst the most heinous positions of spite was that of Amr ibn Saeed ibn Al-Aas, Yazid's agent in Medina. When news came of the martyrdom of Hussain in Medina, the entire city was shaken. You would not see an advocate like the advocates amongst the women of Banu Hashim, in their role in the revolution of Hussain. The daughter of Aqeel ibn Abi Talib went out mournfully along with a number of her women. As she clenched and twisted her clothes she said in verse:

"What would you say if the Prophet told you
What have you done and you are the last of the nations
To hold onto my family and lineage after I pass
But now some are captives and some are soaked in blood"

When Amr ibn Saeed heard them he laughed and mocked them. Al-Tabari, *Tareekh Al-Tabari*, 4:356-357; Ibn Atheer, *Al-Kamil*, 3:300.

groups to take practical steps in opposition to the regime, especially in transforming the common psyche towards the Umayyads.

When the Umayyads realized this new reality, they exerted much effort to battle the psychological impact the revolution had on the nation. The Muslim nation began shifting in its allegiance for the regime to rising against it, its institutions and its policies.

Just as the Umayyad dynasty saw the grave repercussions of its cruel suppression of the revolution, Shia leaders – especially the Imams of Ahlulbayt – saw in the revolution a beam of hope. They recognized that the outcome of the revolution had set the foregrounds for mobilizing the masses against the Umayyads and ridding the nation of their tyrannical rule. This leadership readied itself to confront the Umayyad machine through igniting and flaming the revolution by means of its psychological and spiritual impact on the masses of the nation.

In the next segment we will provide a brief illustration of the Umayyad efforts to undermine the work of the revolution. Then we will delve into a detailed study of the work of the Shia leadership – the foremost being the Imams of Ahlulbayt – that countered Umayyad efforts and aimed to rejuvenate the revolution to turn the people against the Umayyads. At the end, we will see that the true victors were the Shia.

The Popular Conscience

The Umayyads' efforts in suppressing the revolution came in two ways.

The First

One of foremost historical facts surrounding the revolution is that Yazid ibn Muawiya was primarily responsible for what happened in Karbala. With news of the gruesome massacre that took place in Karbala, Yazid was elated. He did not oppose the methods his governor, ibn Ziyad, employed against the revolutionaries. In fact, he was part and parcel of the entire process, a principal in issuing brutal policies against dissenters. However, when the consequences of the massacre were revealed Yazid tried to provide disclaimers and justifications for his actions.

Ubaydillah ibn Ziyad said in a conversation with Musafir ibn Shureih al-Bakri, "In regards to killing Al-Hussain, Yazid threatened me that I either kill Hussain or I will be killed. So, I chose the former."[1]

Historians have stated:

> When the head of Al-Hussain arrived before Yazid, ibn Ziyad grew in Yazid's eyes. Yazid increased his salary, raised his status and praised him for what he had done. His delight was unaffected until he was told of the people's spite of him, and that they damned him and cursed him. Only then did he feel regret over the murder of Al-Hussain.[2]

He also said to Nu'man ibn Basheer Al-Ansari, "Praise be to God who killed Hussain."[3]

The reality of popular dissent pressed the regime's leadership to make attempts at changing the narrative by way of shifting responsibility. They attempted to exonerate the Umayyad establishment, and Yazid specifically, from all blame for the brutal massacre of Imam Hussain at Karbala. Instead, they shifted blame

---

[1] Ibn Al-Atheer, *Al-Kamil*, 4:140.

[2] Ibn Al-Atheer, *Al-Kamil*, 3:300; Al-Suyooti, *Tareekh Al-Khulafa*, 208.

[3] Al-Khawarizmi, *Maqtal Al-Hussain*, 2:59.

to specific individuals in the regime and argued that they were solely and individually responsible for the crimes committed. Blame was shifted particularly to Ubaydillah ibn Ziyad. This attempt would direct the spirit of animosity and indignation against one man, instead of the entire regime. More importantly, it relieved the individual at the helm of state: Yazid ibn Muawiya.

In researching this matter, you will find the effects of these attempts on some of the narrators of tradition like Ibn Hajar Al-Haythami. Ibn Hajar went to the extent to claim that Yazid was not content with the murder of Imam Hussain and did not order his killing either.[4]

It seems that such marketing campaigns and propaganda were central to Iraq and Hijaz[5]. They did not need to include Syria in their target audience, given that the Umayyads had engraved in their tradition that the Day of Ashura was a day of happiness and celebration.

---

[4] Al-Haythami, *Al-Fatawa Al-Hadeetha*, 193, citing *Maqtal Al-Hussain* by Abdil-Razzaq Al-Muqarram.

[5] Hijaz is a region in the west of present-day Saudi Arabia. It is bordered on the west by the Red Sea, on the north by Jordan, on the east by Najd and on the south by Asir.

This attempt essentially failed and public opinion did not exonerate Yazid or the Umayyad regime from the crime they committed.

Some of the contemporary Muslim scholars have continued the Umayyad attempt at vindicating Yazid and thus forbade the mentioning of Yazid ibn Muawiya in any negative light. This is noticeably after the movement of Shia became stronger and more openly expressed itself through the rituals of Ashura.[6] Nonetheless, public opinion stood firmly against this vain attempt and did not bare an effect on the popular conscience of the people. Instead, Yazid remained in the people's conscience as the primary figure of the heinous crime that was the massacre of Karbala.

THE SECOND

The Umayyads also tried to distort the revolution, which was essentially even more dangerous than the first method they employed.

They attempted to distort the revolution in pushing two primary views:

---

[6] The rituals of Ashura are called *Al-Shaa'ir Al-Hussainiya* in Arabic. These rituals include gatherings of recitations, sermons, poetry, elegies, and other forms of remembrance for the tragedy of Imam Hussain.

First, they tried to persuade public opinion that Hussain's rise was driven by his thirst for power. By convincing people of that, the Umayyads would be able to show that the purpose of his revolution was not for the good of Islam but rather was simply driven by his own personal ambitions. Furthermore, when he failed to accomplish what he set out to do, he showed that he was ready to let go of his selfish ambitions and give up.

This is reflected in a narration which relays that Imam Hussain told Umar ibn Saad, "Let us go together to Yazid, so that I may pledge allegiance to him." The outright lie in this narration is seen clearly when comparing it to authentic historical accounts. For example, 'Aqaba ibn Sam'an, who was a helper in Imam Hussain's household and of the very few men to have survived the massacre in Karbala, narrates what he witnessed with his own eyes:

> *I accompanied Hussain from Medina to Mecca and from Mecca to Iraq. I did not leave his side until he was killed. I heard every speech he gave to the people until the day he died. I swear by God, he did not present the options that people accused him of wanting to take. He did not say he would pledge allegiance to Yazid nor did he wish to take refuge in a faraway land of the Islamic empire. Rather he said,*

'let me return to the place that I came from [Medina]'.[7]

This attempt did actually affect some people's perspectives and was successful to an extent, as described by 'Aqaba ibn Sam'an when he said, "I swear by God, he did not present the options that people accused him of wanting to take." However, this attempt failed in realizing success because it came after the accounts of eyewitnesses who refuted and disavowed such accusations.

Second, the Umayyads tried to make Hussain and his supporters out to be Kharijites[8] or hoodlums who defied the law and authority vested in Yazid ibn Muawiya. In their attempt, they wished to portray Hussain and his supporters as instigators who disobeyed their leader and created discord in the community.

From the moment that Ibn Ziyad set foot in Kufa, he wanted to instill the notion that Muslim ibn Aqeel's

---

[7] Al-Tabari, *Tareekh Al-Tabari*, Vol. 5.

[8] The event of Tahkeem gave rise to the Kharijites, a group of Muslims who believed that both Ali ibn Abi Talib and Muawiya should be removed because their decision to appoint arbiters to decide the dispute went against established tradition. The Kharijites amassed an army and prepared to attack Ali ibn Abi Talib. The armies met at Nahrawan (modern day Iraq). Although Ali ibn Abi Talib was victorious in the battle, the remnants of the Kharijites would continue to cause trouble and would ultimately succeed in assassinating Ali ibn Abi Talib.

movement in the city was one created by the Kharijites. There is no doubt that the efforts to label the
revolution of Imam Hussain in this manner were pur-
sued to limit the negative reactions against the regime
within public opinion.

This attempt, however, was not successful in wielding
public opinion in the way the Umayyads wanted. Instead of placing the revolution of Hussain outside of
the law, the Umayyad regime was inadvertently sub-
ject to scrutiny and accused of illegitimacy. Scores of
people began to reject the Umayyads after learning of
the revolution and its vision of truth and justice in
accordance to the ideals of Islam.

The increasing presence of Shiites after the Umayyads
– coupled with the prominence of the Shiites in their
political stances against the regime and the Abbasid's
inclination to nurture the jurisprudential and theologi-
cal perspectives that were opposing to Shia thought –
created a sectarian environment that drove some jurists and theologians to appease the demands of the
zealot rulers or even zealot laymen with some prepos-
terous public acts of sectarianism. Some of the biggest
jurists shed light and unmasked and incriminated
these acts with determination. One of the preposter-
ous sectarian positions was the attempt to give legitimacy to Yazid's actions and the policies of the Umay-

yad regime against the revolution of Al-Hussain. In that they attempted to strip away legitimacy from the revolution. Below we mention some of these specific attempts.

One such position is that of Abu Bakr ibn Arabi in his book *al-'Awasim min al-Qawasim*. He said of al-Hussain,

> No one set out against him [i.e. against al-Hussain] except by some interpretation. They would not have fought him were it not for what they heard from his grandfather, the Seal of the Messengers, who told of the corruption of time and the advent of sedition. His words in this regard are many, including, 'There will be evils and corruption. Whoever wishes to divide the matter of this nation while it is united, strike him with the sword no matter who he was.' People did not set out [against al-Hussain] except by this [tradition] and its likes.[9]

Ibn al-Jawzi wrote in his book *al-Sir al-Masoun*,

> Of the popular believes that have taken hold of a group of those who attribute themselves to the Sunnah is that Yazid was right and that al-Hussain was wrong in setting out against him... Surely, none would ascribe to this view but one who is ignorant of

---

[9] Ibn Arabi, *al-'Awasim min al-Qawasim*, 232.

history and uneducated in creed, who holds such view out of spite for al-Rafida.[10]

Al-Shawkani said,

Some scholars went to the extreme of making the judgment that al-Hussain al-Sibt – may God be pleased with him and please him – had transgressed against the profligate drunkard Yazid ibn Muawiya – may God curse them. What astonishing statements that make the skin crawl and would break any boulder [out of shock]![11]

These statements reflect an antagonistic position to Hussain's revolution in the popular conscience of a small group of Muslims. It was cultivated by Umayyad efforts and propaganda tools. However, this position soon lost its supporters among the Muslim public. Its supporters dwindled. Scholars would mention this view only to put on the record their disagreement and condemnation of such a position. One such scholar in modern times is Imam Sheikh Muhammad Abduh who said,

---

[10] Al-Hanbali, *al-Furu'*, 3:548. Rafida – rejecters – was a title given to the group of individuals who re-jected the legitimacy of the first three caliphs – Abu Bakr, Umar, and Uthman. Thus, followers of the Prophet's Household were seen as those who rejected the three caliphs' legitimacy and authority.

[11] Al-Shawkani, *Nayl al-Awtar*, 147.

> *If there is in the world a just government which es-*
> *tablishes the legislation [of God] and another that is*
> *oppressive and obstructs [the legislation of God], it*
> *becomes obligatory for every Muslim to support the*
> *former... This was the justification of the rise of*
> *Imam Hussain, the grandson of the Messenger (s),*
> *against Yazid ibn Muawiya, the leader of oppres-*
> *sion and deviation who was grasped authority over*
> *the Muslims with force and deception – may God*
> *desert him and those who attempt to justify his ac-*
> *tions, like the Karamiyya and the Nawasib.[12]*

This stance has become a bygone piece of history that
provokes mockery and wonder at these absurd views
whose holders are so unimaginative that they hold on
to the strangest of views. They do so to create some
noise that will gain them what they perceive to be the
fame which they long and strive for to no avail. Their
blind egos lead them to infamy by submerging them
in this Umayyad filth.

The stance that continues to live with vigor is the one
made in the year 61 AH. Its roots continue to run
deep in the popular conscience of all Muslims, and of
Shia Muslims in particular. It is to hold on to revolution, revere it, and seek inspiration from it. It is the

---

[12] Al-Shawkani, *Nayl al-Awtar*, 7:147.

stance of anyone who knows the truth of Hussaini Revolution.